Table of Contents

Introduction

Looking for healthier noodle recipes that aren't bland and boring? If so, you've come to the right place! This recipe book consists of 30 delicious zoodle recipes that will satisfy your taste buds while also cutting out carby noodles.

With this book, you'll be able to put up all sorts of delicious zoodles recipes! All the recipes are detailed, easy-to-follow and versatile in nature and can be made by even the most beginner cook. So, choose a recipe and let's get started!

1. Lentil Zoodle Soup

This hearty and delicious soup is perfect for the colder months.

Makes: 2-3 servings

Prep: 5 mins

Cook: 35 mins

Ingredients:

- 2 teaspoons extra-virgin olive oil
- 1 rib celery, diced
- 2 medium carrots, peeled and diced
- 1 small onion, diced
- 3 cups water, divided

- 3 zucchinis, spiralized into noodles
- 1/2 cup green lentils
- Salt and pepper
- Grated Parmesan cheese, for garnish

Directions:

In a pan, heat the oil. Add in the onion, celery, and carrots, sauté, stirring occasionally, for about 7 minutes. Stir in 2 cups water and the lentils. Bring to a boil, then cover partially so that just a crack remains. Reduce the heat and cook until lentils are soft, about 20 minutes.

Add the remaining 1 cup of water and bring to a simmer over medium heat. Add the zoodles to the soup. Simmer until the zoodles are tender, about 3 minutes. Season to taste with salt and pepper. Serve with Parmesan cheese sprinkled on top.

2. Shrimp and Garlic Zoodles

Delicious garlicky zoodles made with shrimp and broccoli.

Makes: 3 servings

Prep: 5 mins

Cook: 15 mins

Ingredients:

- 3 zucchinis, spiralized into noodles
- 1 Tbsp. vegetable oil

- 1 lb. shrimp
- Kosher salt
- Black pepper
- 1 Tbsp. sesame oil
- 2 cloves minced garlic
- 1 tsp. minced ginger
- ½ cup soy sauce
- ¼ cup brown sugar
- Juice of 1 lime
- 2 tsp. Sriracha
- 1 cup vegetable broth
- 1 large broccoli head, cut into florets
- 1 red bell pepper, thinly sliced
- 2 green onions, thinly sliced

Directions:

In a pan, heat the oil over med heat.

Season the shrimp with salt and pepper and cook for approximately 2 minutes on each side until they become opaque and pink. Once cooked, remove the shrimp from the frying pan and set them to one side.

Turn the heat down to low and add in the sesame oil.

Add the ginger garlic and cook for 1 minute. Add in the Sriracha, lime juice, vegetable broth, brown sugar, and soy sauce.

Increase heat and bring to a boil. Once boiling, lower the heat down and allow the sauce to simmer until it starts to thicken; approximately 5 minutes.

Add the bell peppers and broccoli and cover the frying pan with a lid. Cook the vegetables until they become tender; approximately 5 minutes.

Add the shrimp to the pan stir until they are coated with the sauce. Add the green onions and the zoodles and stir.

Immediately serve with the Sriracha.

3. Garlic, Butter and Parmesan Zoodles

A simple 4-ingredient zoodle recipe with garlic, butter and parmesan.

Makes: 3 servings

Prep: 5 mins

Cook: 5 mins

Ingredients:

- 3 Tbsp. butter
- ¼ cup parmesan
- 2 cloves garlic

- 3 zucchinis, spiralized into noodles
- 2 Tbsp. flat leaf parsley, chopped

Directions:

Melt the butter in a non-stick pan. Add in the garlic and sauté for 1 minute. Add the zoodles and the parmesan and stir to combine.

Divide between bowls, garnish with parsley serve.

4. Chicken Zoodle Soup

A hearty and comforting chicken zoodle soup with peas and carrots.

Makes: 4 servings

Prep: 5 mins

Cook: 5 mins

Ingredients:

- 5 cups water
- 3 zucchinis, spiralized into noodles
- 2 cups snow peas, sliced diagonally

- 2 green onions, sliced
- 1 large carrot, shredded
- 1 pound chicken breast
- 1 tsp. Asian sesame oil

Directions:

Heat the water in a large saucepan.

Cut the chicken into bite size pieces.

Once the water and the seasoning have boiled, add the zoodles, chicken, carrot, green onions, and snow peas. Cook over high heat for approximately 5 mins.

Take off the heat, add the sesame oil, divide into bowls and then serve.

5. Spinach Zoodle Breakfast Bowl

Before you dig into this satisfying breakfast, break the yolk of the fried egg and stir it into the zoodles. The zoodles are flavored with seaweed seasoning, made of dried seaweed, sesame seeds, salt, and other flavorings.

Makes: 1 serving

Prep: 5 mins

Cook: 10 mins

Ingredients:

- 1/2 cup chopped spinach, frozen or fresh
- 2 zucchinis, spiralized into noodles
- 1 tablespoon soy sauce
- 1 teaspoon seaweed seasoning
- 1 tablespoon unsalted butter
- 1 large egg

Directions:

Boil water in a pot over medium-high heat. Add the spinach and boil for 3 minutes. Drain and return to the pot. Add the zoodles, soy sauce and the seasoning and stir to combine.

In a skillet set over med-high heat, melt the butter until it foams. Break the egg into the pan and let it cook, undisturbed, until the white is completely firm but the yolk is still liquid, about 3 minutes. If desired, flip the egg over after about 2 minutes.

To serve, transfer the seasoned zoodles and spinach into a bowl and top with the fried egg.

6. Japanese Chicken-Zoodle Soup

This soup is so thick and chunky you could eat it with chopsticks. This is a variation of the nábemono (things in a pot) from Japan. It's a full-dish meal and has traditional Japanese visual appeal with a combination of colors and shapes.

Makes: 4 servings

Prep: 5 mins

Cook: 5 mins

Ingredients:

- 2 chicken breasts, boned and skinned
- 1 egg white
- 1 tablespoon cornstarch
- 1 tablespoon sake or dry white wine
- 4 cups chicken broth
- 1 cup water
- 2 teaspoons GF soy sauce

- 3 zucchinis, spiralized into noodles
- 1 cup carrots, sliced diagonally
- 6 Napa cabbage leaves, in 2-inch squares
- 6 green onions, in 1-inch lengths
- 8 mushrooms, sliced (shiitake or button)

Directions:

Wash chicken breasts and slice into thin slivers; combine with the egg white, cornstarch, and sake. Set aside.

In a large kettle, bring the chicken broth, water, and soy sauce to boil. Add zoodles to the broth. Cook for about 4 minutes. Add the carrots, cabbage, onions, and mushrooms. Cook until carrots are tender. Stir in the chicken and cook for 1 to 2 minutes. Serve Japanese style in deep bowls with large ceramic spoons.

7. Bacon, Egg, and Zoodle Scramble

A quick, easy and satisfying breakfast recipe. Add a cup of coffee and a wedge or two of cantaloupe and you're set.

Makes: 1 serving

Prep: 5 mins

Cook: 20 mins

Ingredients:

- 3 zucchinis, spiralized into noodles
- 2 strips bacon
- 1/2 tablespoon unsalted butter
- 2 large eggs
- 1 ounce cheddar or Colby cheese, shredded (about 2 tablespoons)
- Salt and pepper

Directions:

Put the bacon in a skillet and heat the pan over medium-high heat. Cook the bacon until crisp, 7 to 10 minutes, turning over as needed to evenly cook both sides. Remove the bacon from the pan drain any excess fat if necessary, so there's no more than about 1 teaspoon of bacon fat left. When the bacon cools, crumble it into pieces and set aside.

Add the butter to the hot pan with the bacon fat. When the butter melts, add the zoodles and cook, stirring frequently, for 3 to 4 mins. Meanwhile, beat the 2 eggs in a bowl with a fork or a whisk. Reduce the heat to low and add the eggs to the pan. Cook, stirring, until the eggs are nearly scrambled, about 4 minutes. Sprinkle the cheese over the eggs and cook, stirring frequently, until the cheese melts. Transfer to a plate, season to taste with salt and pepper, sprinkle the crumbled bacon on top, and serve.

8. Miso Zoodles

Serve this with a grilled-cheese sandwich for a nice lunch.

Makes: 2 servings

Prep: 3 mins

Cook: 5 mins

Ingredients:

- 2 cups water
- 1 package miso soup mix
- 2 scallions, chopped
- 1/2 cup diced soft tofu
- 1/4 cup sliced cremini mushrooms or shiitakes with stems

discarded (optional)

- 3 zucchinis, spiralized into noodles

Directions:

In a saucepan, bring 2 cups of the water to a low simmer. Add the soup mix, scallions, tofu, and mushrooms, if using, and stir to combine. Add the zoodles and simmer for 3 minutes. Serve immediately.

9. Beef Ginger Zoodle Stir-Fry

Delightful zoodle stir fry with beef and ginger.

Makes: 4 servings

Prep: 5 mins

Cook: 10 mins

Ingredients:

- 3 zucchinis, spiralized into noodles
- ¾ cup soy sauce, low sodium
- 1 Tbsp. rice ginger
- 1 clove minced garlic
- 2 inches minced fresh ginger
- 1 tsp. red chili flakes
- 1 pound flank steak, sliced
- ¼ pounds trimmed beans
- Vegetable oil

Directions:

Combine the red chili flakes, garlic, ginger, rice vinegar, and soy sauce in a bowl and whisk together thoroughly.

Heat some oil in a large frying.

Add the steak and cook for 4 minutes per side. Remove the steak from the pan and allow it to rest on a chopping board. Slice.

Add the green beans, carrots and the soy sauce mixture to the frying pan and stir together thoroughly. Allow the ingredients to simmer until they become tender.

Add the zoodles and the beef and cook for a further 3 minutes.

Divide into bowls and serve.

10. Zoodle Casserole

Zoodle casserole with beef, tomatoes and cheese.

Makes: 8 servings

Prep: 5 mins

Cook: 40 mins

Ingredients:

- 1 can of diced tomatoes
- 3 cups of warm water
- 8 zucchinis, spiralized into noodles
- 2 cups of lean ground beef
- 1 finely diced onion
- Velveeta cheese

Directions:

Preheat the oven to 200 degrees C.

In a pan, cook the beef and the onions for 10 minutes or until browned. Add the tomatoes and water and boil the mixture for 5 minutes. Lastly, add the zoodles and cook for a further 5 minutes.

Transfer the Ingredients into a large casserole dish, top with desired amount of cheese and bake for 15 mins or until all the cheese has completely melted.

Divide into bowls and serve.

11. Herby Buttered Zoodles and Peas

Sometimes simple is best, as is this comforting, buttery zoodle dish that is delicious alongside an easy frozen or prepared food like a rotisserie chicken or fish sticks.

Makes: 2 servings

Prep: 2 mins

Cook: 5 mins

Ingredients:

- 3 zucchinis, spiralized into noodles
- 1 cup frozen peas
- 2 tablespoons unsalted butter, diced

- 2 tablespoons chopped fresh parsley
- Salt and pepper

Directions:

Cook the zoodles and peas in boiling water for 3 minutes. Drain and return to the pot.

Immediately add the butter, tossing the zoodles to coat completely. Sprinkle with the parsley season to taste with salt and pepper. Serve immediately

12. Zoodles with Wild Mushrooms and Parmesan Sauce

This recipe entails wild mushrooms, sautéed and served atop zoodles which is in turn dressed in a creamy Alfredo-type sauce.

Makes: 4 servings

Prep: 5 mins

Cook: 25 mins

Ingredients:

- 1 tablespoon extra-virgin olive oil
- 6 ounces mixed wild mushrooms, stemmed where needed, and sliced
- Salt and pepper

- 2 tablespoons unsalted butter
- 2 tablespoons flour
- 1 1/2 cups milk
- 1/2 cup grated Parmesan cheese
- 1/8 teaspoon ground nutmeg
- 3 zucchinis, spiralized into noodles

Directions:

In a skillet, heat the olive oil. Add the mushrooms and sauté for 8 minutes or until the mushrooms are soft and browned. Season with salt and pepper, and transfer to a bowl. Cover loosely with aluminum foil to keep warm.

In a small saucepan, melt the butter over medium-low heat. When the butter foams, whisk in the flour and continue whisking until a thick paste is formed. Gradually whisk in the milk, whisking between additions until the mixture is lump-free. When all of the milk has been added, bring it to a simmer and cook, stirring occasionally, until the sauce has thickened, about 5 minutes. Stir in the Parmesan cheese and the nutmeg and cook until the cheese has melted and the sauce is smooth and creamy, about 5 minutes.

Add the zoodles to the pot. Add the Parmesan sauce and stir to coat.

To serve, divide the zoodles among four bowls. Top each bowl with a spoonful of mushrooms and a sprinkling of Parmesan cheese.

13. Zoodles with Cherry Tomatoes and Mozzarella

This quick zoodles dish has a no-cook sauce that's particularly tasty in the summer when tomatoes are at their best.

Makes: 2 servings

Prep: 10 mins

Cook: 5 mins

Ingredients:

- 1 cup cherry tomatoes, quartered
- 1 tablespoon chopped Kalamata olives
- 2 tablespoons chopped fresh basil
- 4 ounces fresh mozzarella, diced
- 2 tablespoons extra-virgin olive oil
- Salt and pepper
- 2 zucchinis, spiralized into noodles
- 2 tablespoons grated Parmesan cheese

Directions:

In a bowl, combine the olives, tomatoes, basil, and mozzarella. Drizzle with the olive oil and stir to combine. Season to taste with the salt pepper.

Add zoodles to the pot. Add the tomato mix stir to combine. Divide the mixture between two plates or shallow bowls and sprinkle with the Parmesan cheese.

14. Zoodles Alfredo with Asparagus

The asparagus in this recipe cuts through the rich and decadent Alfredo sauce leaving you with a wonderfully balanced meal.

Makes: 2 servings

Prep: 5 mins

Cook: 10 mins

Ingredients:

- 1 cup heavy cream
- 4 tablespoons unsalted butter, cut into pieces
- 1/2 cup Parmesan cheese
- 1/2 teaspoon garlic powder

- pinch of nutmeg
- black pepper
- 3 zucchinis, spiralized into noodles
- 1 cup chopped fresh or frozen asparagus (1-inch pieces)

Directions:

In a saucepan, put the cream to a simmer over medium heat. Add the butter and stir occasionally until completely melted. Add the cheese, garlic powder, and nutmeg. Simmer over med-low heat, stirring frequently, until the cheese is melted and the mixture is smooth and creamy, about 5 minutes. Season to taste with pepper.

Add zoodles to the pot. Stir in the sauce to coat the zoodles completely. To serve, divide the zoodles between two bowls and sprinkle with additional Parmesan cheese.

15. Cilantro Pesto Zoodles

The bracing flavor of cilantro is toned down when it's combined with the traditional ingredients in pesto: Parmesan cheese, olive oil, and garlic.

Makes: 2 servings

Prep: 5 mins

Cook: 5 mins

Ingredients:

- 2 1/2 cups fresh cilantro (from 1 large bunch)
- 1 clove garlic, coarsely chopped
- 1/4 cup grated Parmesan cheese
- 1/2 cup chopped walnuts
- 1/4 cup extra-virgin olive oil
- lime juice
- Salt and pepper
- 3 zucchinis, spiralized into noodles

Directions:

In a food processor, put the cilantro and garlic and pulse. Add the Parmesan cheese and the walnuts and pulse to puree to combine the ingredients well. Slowly drizzle in the olive oil through the feed tube until the mixture makes a loose paste.

Transfer to a bowl season to taste with lime juice, salt, and pepper. Cover by pressing plastic wrap against the surface of the pesto to keep it from browning and set aside.

Add the zoodles to the pot and toss with several generous spoonfuls of the pesto to coat well while still hot.

16. Sesame Zoodles

Here's a basic, all-purpose zoodle dish that's not meant to be eaten on its own. Instead, it's a subtly flavorful base for stir-fries, curries, sautéed vegetables etc.

Makes: 2 servings

Prep: 5 mins

Cook: 3 mins

Ingredients:

- 3 zucchinis, spiralized into noodles
- 2 teaspoons sesame oil
- 1 tablespoon sesame seeds

Directions:

Add zoodles to a pot. Drizzle the zoodles with the sesame oil and sprinkle with sesame seeds, and toss. Heat for 2 mins and then serve.

17. Zoodle Bolognese

Sometimes a little red-sauce pasta is just what you need.

Makes: 2 servings

Prep: 5 mins

Cook: 25 mins

Ingredients:

- 1 tablespoon extra-virgin olive oil
- 1 small onion, diced
- 1 clove garlic, minced
- 4 ounces ground turkey or ground beef
- 1 (15-ounce) can crushed tomatoes
- 1 tablespoon tomato paste
- 1 tablespoon dried Italian herbs
- Salt and pepper

- 3 zucchinis, spiralized into noodles
- Grated Parmesan cheese, for serving

Directions:

In a saucepan, heat the olive oil. Add the onion and sauté for about 5 minutes. Add in the garlic and stir for 1 min. Add the beef/turkey and cook, breaking up the large chunks, until the meat is browned cooked through, 5 to 7 minutes. Tilt the pan and remove excess oil or cooking liquid.

Stir in the tomatoes, tomato paste, and Italian herbs. Bring to a boil. Lower cook for 15 minutes to allow the flavors to meld. Season to taste with salt and pepper.

While the sauce is simmering, cook zoodles for 2 mins. Serve with Bolognese sauce and sprinkle with Parmesan cheese.

18. Stir-Fried Vegetables in Coconut-Ginger Sauce

Zoodles soak up the delicate, subtly sweet coconut sauce in this surprisingly simple recipe. Use a package of frozen stir-fry vegetables or any combination of your favorite fresh or frozen veggies.

Makes: 2 servings

Prep: 5 mins

Cook: 20 mins

Ingredients:

- 1 tablespoon vegetable or canola oil
- 2 cups frozen stir-fry vegetables
- 1 clove garlic, minced
- 1 teaspoon minced ginger
- 3/4 cup coconut milk
- Juice of 1 lime
- 1 teaspoon soy sauce
- Pinch of red pepper flakes
- 3 zucchinis, spiralized into noodles

Directions:

Heat the oil in a skillet. Add the veggies and cook for about 5 to 7 minutes. Add the garlic and ginger and cook, stirring constantly, for 30 seconds. Add the coconut milk and simmer over medium-high heat, stirring occasionally, until the sauce is slightly thickened, 5 to 7 minutes. Season to taste with the juice, soy sauce, red pepper flakes. Add zoodles to the pot and cook for 2 mins. Serve.

19. Cabbage Zoodle Salad

Zoodles with cabbage, sunflower seeds and vinegar.

Makes: 6 servings

Prep: 5 mins

Cook: 4 mins

Ingredients:

- 3 tbsp. white sugar
- ½ cup sunflower seeds
- ½ cup vegetable oil
- ½ large head cabbage, finely chopped
- 3 zucchinis, spiralized into noodles
- 3 tbsp. distilled white vinegar

Directions:

In a med-sized bowl, combine the oil, sugar, ramen seasoning, and vinegar.

Cook zoodles for 2 mins.

In a separate bowl, combine the zoodles, sunflower seeds and cabbage.

Pour the vinegar mixture on top of the salad and stir to combine.

Divide into bowls and serve.

20. Iced Kimchi Zoodles

Iced kimchi zoodles recipe with beef tenderloin and broth.

Makes: 4 servings

Prep: 20 mins

Cook: 20 mins

Ingredients:

BROTH:

- 2 cups (470 ml) store-bought beef broth, preferably unsalted
- 2 cups (470 ml) water
- 1 tablespoon fish sauce
- 1 tablespoon sugar
- 1 small beef tenderloin (about ¾ pound/340 g)
- 1 cup (150 g) napa cabbage kimchi
- ¼ cup (60 ml) kimchi juice
- 1 cup (235 ml) ice water

- 3 tablespoons rice vinegar

TOPPINGS:

- 1 English cucumber or 2 Persian cucumbers
- 1 Asian pear
- 2 hard-boiled eggs
- Salt

ZOODLES:

- 3 zucchinis, spiralized into noodles

GARNISH:

- Finely chopped scallions
- Toasted sesame seeds
- Sesame oil

Directions:

Make the broth: Combine the beef broth, water, fish sauce, and sugar in a medium saucepan over high heat. Bring to boil, and then add the beef tenderloin and reduce the heat to maintain a gentle simmer. Cover with a lid on the saucepan and cook the beef until well done (170°F/77°C on an instant-read thermometer), about 18 minutes. Transfer the beef to a plate; cover and refrigerate until chilled.

Squeeze the kimchi over a small bowl to catch the juices. Add enough juice from the jar to make up ¼ cup (60 ml). Finely chop the kimchi; set it aside until you are ready to serve.

Stir in the kimchi juice, ice water, and rice vinegar, and place the broth in the freezer to cool.

Prepare the toppings: While the beef and the broth are cooling, prepare the remaining toppings. Julienne the cucumber, core the pear and slice it as thinly as you can, and peel and halve the hardboiled eggs.

When the beef is cool to the touch, slice it thinly across the grain. Set all the toppings aside until you are ready to serve.

Assemble the bowls: Cook the zoodles for a few minutes until tender. Fan a few slices of beef tenderloin over each portion, then add kimchi, pear slices, julienned cucumber, and half an egg.

Take the broth out of the freezer taste it for seasoning; add salt if it needs it. Carefully ladle the broth into the bowls, taking care not to disturb the toppings. Garnish with chopped scallions, a sprinkle of toasted sesame seeds, and a small drizzle of sesame oil.

21. Beef and Scallion Zoodles

This simple recipe has a light soy-lime sauce that goes well with the beef and scallions. It's a perfect topping for Sesame Ramen zoodles, or even just on plain zoodles.

Makes: 1 serving

Prep: 5 mins

Cook: 10 mins

Ingredients:

- 1/4 cup soy sauce
- 1 tablespoon lime juice
- 1 teaspoon sesame oil
- 4 ounces flank steak or skirt steak, thinly sliced
- 6 scallions, halved lengthwise and cut diagonally into 1-inch pieces
- 3 zucchinis, spiralized into noodles

- 1 tablespoon vegetable oil
- 1 teaspoon cornstarch

Directions:

In a bowl, put together the sesame oil, soy sauce, lime juice. Add the steak and the scallions and marinate for 5 minutes.

While the steak marinates, cook the zoodles for 2-3 mins.

Heat the oil in a skillet. With a fork/slotted spoon, remove the steak and the scallions from the marinade, reserving the marinade, and add the meat and the scallions to the pan. Cook, stirring frequently, until the steak is browned and the scallions are softened, 2 to 3 minutes. Whisk the cornstarch into the marinade and pour it into the pan. Bring to a boil. Cook for about 1 minute. Serve on a bed of zoodles.

22. Chilly Ginger-Cucumber Salad

Cool and refreshing, this simple salad makes a great accompaniment to homemade sushi, grilled tuna, or fried chicken.

Makes: 2-4 servings

Prep: 5 mins

Cook: 3 mins

Ingredients:

- 1/4 cup rice vinegar
- 1 teaspoon grated fresh ginger
- 1 teaspoon canola oil

- 3 zucchinis, spiralized into noodles
- 1 cucumber, peeled, seeded, and diced
- 1 scallion, light green dark green parts only, sliced
- 1 tablespoon sesame seeds

Directions:

In a serving bowl, combine together the vinegar, ginger, and canola oil.

Add in zoodles to the bowl toss with the cucumber and scallion to coat all the ingredients well with the dressing. Sprinkle with the sesame seeds. Serve immediately.

23. Spicy Beef and Mushroom Stew

This hearty, beefy stew has an addictively spicy edge.

Makes: 2 servings

Prep: 5 mins

Cook: 25 mins

Ingredients:

- 2 teaspoons extra-virgin olive oil
- 1/2 onion, cut in half and sliced
- 1 rib celery, thinly sliced
- 1 carrot, peeled, halved lengthwise, and thinly sliced
- 1 cup quartered cremini or white mushrooms

- 6 ounces flank steak or hanger steak, cut into bite-size pieces
- 1 tablespoon balsamic vinegar
- 1 cup beef stock or broth
- 1 cup water
- 3 zucchinis, spiralized into noodles

Directions:

Heat the oil in a saucepan. Add the onion, celery, and carrot and sauté, stirring occasionally, until the vegetables are softened, about 5 minutes. Add the mushrooms and steak and sauté, stirring, until the steak is browned and the mushrooms are soft, 2 to 3 minutes.

Add the stock or broth, water, and ramen seasoning. Bring to a simmer, then reduce the heat to low and simmer for 10 minutes. Add the zoodles in and cook until soft, about 3 minutes. Serve immediately.

24. Eggy Sausage Zoodles

This is perfect for the morning after a late night out. It's quick and easy to make and is the perfect combination of richness, spiciness, and deliciousness.

Makes: 1 serving

Prep: 2 mins

Cook: 10 mins

Ingredients:

- 2 zucchinis, spiralized into noodles
- 1 tablespoon unsalted butter
- 1 large egg
- 2 sausage patties, cooked

* Salt and pepper

Directions:

Cook the zoodles for 2 ½ mins. Add in the butter egg, stirring to coat the zoodles with the egg until it is cooked. If there isn't enough heat in the zoodles, you can turn the burner back on and cook the mixture over low heat. Stir in the sausage patties, and season to taste with the salt and pepper. Serve immediately.

25. Mushroom and Egg Zoodles

Mushroom, eggs and zoodles recipe for a delicious breakfast, lunch or dinner.

Makes: 1 serving

Prep: 2 mins

Cook: 10 mins

Ingredients:

- 2 zucchinis, spiralized into noodles
- 1 tablespoon unsalted butter
- 1 large egg
- 1 cup mushrooms, sliced
- Salt and pepper

Directions:

Cook the zoodles and mushrooms for 2 ½ mins or until tender. Add in the butter and egg, stirring to coat the zoodles with the egg until it is cooked. If there isn't enough heat in the zoodles, you can turn the burner back on and cook the mixture over low heat. Season to taste with the salt pepper. Serve immediately.

26. Kale Zoodle Breakfast Bowl

Start your day right with delicious kale zoodle breakfast bowl.

Makes: 1 serving

Prep: 5 mins

Cook: 10 mins

Ingredients:

- 1/2 cup chopped kale, frozen or fresh
- 2 zucchinis, spiralized into noodles
- 1 tablespoon soy sauce
- 1 teaspoon seaweed seasoning
- 1 tablespoon unsalted butter
- 1 large egg

Directions:

Boil water in a pot over medium-high heat. Add the kale and boil for 3 minutes. Drain and return to the pot. Add the zoodles, soy sauce and the seasoning and stir to combine.

In a skillet set over med-high heat, melt the butter until it foams. Break the egg into the pan and let it cook, undisturbed, until the white is completely firm but the yolk is still liquid, about 3 minutes. If desired, flip the egg over after about 2 minutes.

To serve, transfer the seasoned zoodles and kale into a bowl and top with the fried egg.

27. Thai Shrimp Noodle Soup

This delicious Thai noodle soup is super delicious and easy to make!

Makes: 2 servings

Prep: 20 mins

Cook: 15 miss

Ingredients:

- 3 tbsp. peeled and very thinly slivered fresh ginger
- 10 oz. medium-size shrimp, peeled and deveined
- 2 ½ tbsp. fish sauce or soy sauce
- 3 carrots, thinly sliced
- 2 cloves garlic, finely minced
- 2 tsp chopped fresh basil
- 3 cups coarsely chopped fresh spinach
- 10 cups water
- 4 zucchinis, spiralized into noodles
- 4 green onions, minced

- 2 tbsp. Thai hot chili sauce
- 1 cup sliced mushrooms
- Juice and grated zest from 1 ½ limes

Directions:

Fill a large pot with water. Bring this water to a boil on a high flame.

Add the carrots, fish sauce, green onions, ginger, garlic, basil and chili sauce.

Add in the zoodles and boil for 4 minutes or so.

After this, add the shrimp, mushrooms and spinach. Cook for another 5 minutes.

Top with lime zest and juice and stir well.

28. Shredded Lamb with Zoodles

This simple dish combines lamb and zoodles in an easy way.

Makes: 4 servings

Prep: 10 mins

Cook: 20 mins

Ingredients:

- 4 zucchinis, spiralized into noodles
- 7 oz lamb fillet, cut into thin pieces
- 1 beaten egg
- 1 tbsp cornstarch

- ½ tsp salt
- 2 tbsp water
- 2 tbsp peanut oil
- 3 tbsp soy sauce
- 3 spring onions, green only, cut into 2 in lengths
- 1 cup chicken stock
- 1 tsp sesame oil

Directions:

Combine egg, cornstarch, salt and water in a bowl. Coat lamb and leave aside for 10 to 15 minutes.

In a large wok, heat peanut oil and stir fry lamb for 1 or 2 minutes. Add soy and spring onion. Add stock, zoodles, sesame oil and cook for another couple of minutes. Serve warm!

29. Curry Zoodles

The Japanese have adopted the idea of curry in much the same way they adopted the art of deep frying from the Portuguese, and the art of crumbing from eastern Europe. Curry powder first came to Japan in the late 19th century and, while in no way resembling Indian cookery, Japanese curries have a peculiar charm all their own.

Makes: 4 servings

Prep: 10 mins

Cook: 10 mins

Ingredients:

- 4 zucchinis, spiralized into noodles
- 2 tbsp peanut oil
- 2 onions, sliced
- 11 oz boned, chicken thigh, cut into bite-size cubes
- 1 cup green beans, blanched
- 2 tsp curry powder

- 4 cups chicken stock
- 1 tsp sugar
- 2 tbsp tapioca starch or potato starch
- 2 spring onions, finely sliced

Directions:

Heat oil and fry onion gently for a couple of minutes. Add chicken and cook for 1 minute, then add beans and cook for another minute. Sprinkle on curry powder and mix in with a wooden spoon. Pour in stock and sugar, bring to the boil and simmer for 3 minutes. Mix tapioca starch with a little water. Drizzle mixture into the pot, stirring thoroughly. Cook until it begins to boil and starts to thicken.

Pour boiling water over zoodles in a colander or strainer in the sink. Drain well and distribute warmed zoodles among 4 individual bowls. Pour sauce over zoodles and scatter with spring onion.

30. Bang Bang Chicken Zoodles

Poached chicken in a nutty, sweet, chilli sauce with zoodles.

Makes: 4 servings

Prep: 10 mins

Cook: 10 mins

Ingredients:

- 4 zucchinis, spiralized into noodles
- 2 tsp sesame oil
- 1 chicken, about 2 ½ lb.
- 2 spring onions, green part only, finely sliced

Sauce

- 1 tsp sesame seeds

- 2½ tbsp Chinese sesame paste or smooth peanut butter
- 1 tbsp chilli bean sauce
- 2 tbsp cooked peanut oil (heated, then cooled)
- 2 tsp sesame oil
- 1 tbsp sugar
- 1 tbsp soy sauce
- 1½ tbsp Chinese black vinegar
- 2 tbsp chicken stock

Directions:

Pour boiling water over zoodles in a heatproof bowl and let stand for 3 to 5 minutes. Drain. Cut zoodles roughly with a pair of scissors and toss with 1 teaspoon sesame oil.

Lightly toast sesame seeds in a dry, hot pan.

Make sauce by combining sesame paste, chilli bean sauce, cooked peanut oil and sesame oil until it forms a paste. Stir in sugar, soy sauce, black vinegar and chicken stock, and sprinkle sesame seeds on top. Set aside.

Put chicken in a saucepan with a snug–fitting lid and just cover with cold water. Remove chicken and bring water to the boil. Return chicken to the water, reduce heat until water is barely simmering, and cover tightly. Simmer for 30 minutes.

Remove chicken from the saucepan and plunge into a large bowl of icy–cold water. Lift out and replunge three or four times, which will give the chicken a marvelously smooth texture. Brush chicken with remaining teaspoon sesame oil. Remove chicken meat from bones and shred finely.

Put zoodles on a large serving plate. Arrange shredded chicken on top, and pour on the sauce, serving any extra sauce in a small bowl for dipping. Scatter with spring onion and serve.

Conclusion

Well, there you go! 30 delicious ways for you to enjoy zoodles! Make sure you try out each and every recipe. By the end of this, you won't even miss noodles! Also, remember to share with your friends and family!